Snowdonia Slate

a story in photographs

Des Marshall

Gwasg Carreg Gwalch

First published in 2019
© text: Des Marshall
© images: Crown copyright Visit Wales;
Des Marshall; Gwasg Carreg Gwalch

ISBN: 978-1-84524-291-6
Cover design: Eleri Owen

Published by Gwasg Carreg Gwalch,
12 Iard yr Orsaf, Llanrwst, Wales LL26 0EH
tel: 01492 642031
email: books@carreg-gwalch.cymru
website: www.carreg-gwalch.cymru

Acknowledgements
The publisher is grateful to Visit Wales for
photographs on pages 1, 2, 6, 9, 10, 11, 12, 13, 18,
21, 22, 28-29, 36-37, 41, 42, 43, 44-45, 50-51, 62-
63, 74, 75, 86-87, 100-101, 107, 117, 118, 119, 121
and 125, crown copyright.

Map on page 4 by Alison Davies Mapping Co.
Ltd.

*Page 1: View of part of remains of Rhosydd
slate quarry with Cnicht in background
Below: Slate fence and spoil tip Rhosydd
slate quarry*

Contents

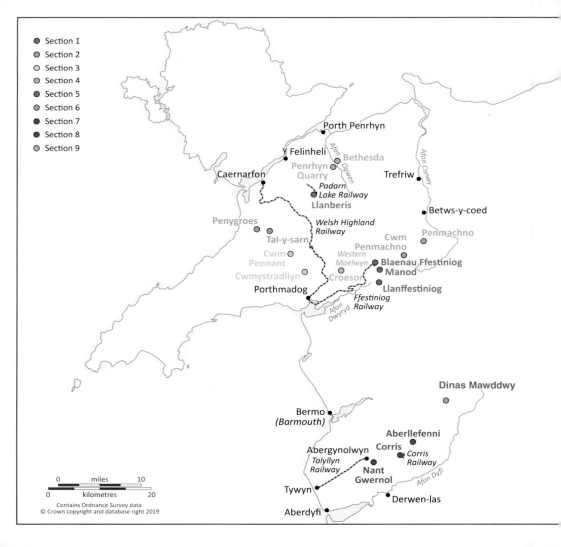

- Section 1
- Section 2
- Section 3
- Section 4
- Section 5
- Section 6
- Section 7
- Section 8
- Section 9

Porth Penrhyn

Y Felinheli

Bethesda

Afon Ogwen

Penrhyn Quarry

Caernarfon

Trefriw

Afon Conwy

Padarn Lake Railway

Llanberis

Betws-y-coed

Penygroes

Welsh Highland Railway

Penmachno

Tal-y-sarn

Cwm Penmachno

Cwm Pennant

Western Moelwyn

Blaenau Ffestiniog

Cwmystradllyn

Croesor

Manod

Porthmadog

Llanffestiniog

Afon Dwyryd

Ffestiniog Railway

Dinas Mawddwy

Bermo *(Barmouth)*

Aberllefenni

Corris

Abergynolwyn

Talyllyn Railway

Corris Railway

Nant Gwernol

Afon Dyfi

Tywyn

Derwen-las

Aberdyfi

0 — miles — 10
0 — kilometres — 20

Contains Ordnance Survey data
© Crown copyright and database right 2019

Introduction

The aim of this book is to illustrate and record the current surface remains of some of the abandoned slate mines and quarries of Snowdonia. It is not exhaustive as there are over 500 quarries and mines, as well as early surface scratchings, in the area. Only the main mines and quarries with the more recognisable remains are recorded herein. Short notes on the quarries or mines have been included. I have done this before what can be seen today disintegrates further at the hands of nature or vandals. I also feel that the Snowdonia slate areas are a big part of its heritage and needs to be conserved. Quarrying and mining slate was once a booming industry that added much to the local economy and has been dubbed "the most 'Welshest' of industries". There is still some small scale quarrying done today notably at Graig Ddu, Maenofferen and Moel Tryfan.

Spoil heaps are often the only vestige of this proud industry but there are still some that have the remains of buildings, such as barracks and waliau; drum houses;

Slatemakers at Llechwedd today

tramways; railway lines and of course remarkable inclines. Fortunately many of the remains are indeed quite substantial. The majority of the mines and quarries are situated on the edge of the Snowdonia National Park but are intertwined into the history of Snowdonia having played an integral part in the history of the area. These are the quarries at Nantlle with the main ones being Tal-y-sarn, Dorothea, Pen y Bryn and Pen yr Orsedd, Above Llanberis is Glynrhonwy and the associated quarries of Cefn-du. Oddly both Dinorwig and Vivian close to Llanberis are outside of the park boundary! Also outside of the park boundary is the huge quarry at Bethesda, Penrhyn. It was once the largest in Wales if not the world.

Towns such as Llanberis, Bethesda, Blaenau Ffestiniog, Bangor, Caernarfon and Porthmadog were created by and owe their existence to the slate industry. Indeed where Blaenau Ffestiniog stands today there were only green fields in 1820. Villages such as Corris, Tal-y-sarn, Penygroes, Dolwyddelan, Dinorwig and Deiniolen also evolved and thrived as a result. Because of the demise of the slate

Ruined machinery and buildings at Rhosydd slate quarry with Cnicht in background

industry many of these towns and villages are now mere shadows of their former glory. Nowadays much of the history of these places has now been relegated to the past and forgotten about with little or no thought or regard about preserving or even conserving any of what does remain. That is a very sad reflection of the toil and hardship the quarrymen and miners experienced whilst putting their lives at risk to obtain slate. Tourism in the area is the modern day equivalent to the slate industry.

A waste tip towering above a part of Blaenau Ffestiniog

This book is not intended to be a walking guide. There are books that do describe walks and trails to many of the quarries and mines. *The Snowdonia Slate Trail* is an 85 miles long walk around the major quarrying and mining areas of northern Snowdonia. It is superbly described in the guide by Aled Owen. Another book describes day walks to many of the mines and quarries in Snowdonia and is titled *Great Walks Exploring Snowdonia's Slate Heritage* written by the author. Another, also by myself, is a guide describing day walks from the actual 'Slate Trail' itself to give a greater and fuller understanding of the slate industry. This is titled *Day walks from the Slate Trail*. These walks follow paths and tracks on public rights of way and do not venture underground. If you feel tempted to look at these remains be mindful that some of these quarries and mines are situated in bleak surroundings high up on a mountainside. Therefore it is important to have the right clothing and footwear for the conditions prevailing. Take note of the recommendations in the guidebooks.

I have given map references to the quarries and mines but please bear in mind that they are very dangerous places. It is definitely most unwise to venture underground without an experienced and qualified guide. There are many areas of loose rock on the walls and floors along with dangerous ceilings. Mines used for commercial exploration are checked by mining engineers who give a report on their suitability of this activity for the various companies that specialise in these trips. It is NOT recommended to venture on to the spoil heaps. They are loose and can be very slippery especially in the wet when a layer of lichen acts like soap. Please be aware that slate is also extremely sharp and can cause nasty cuts and lacerations. If you want to experience more things slate I have included a list of other attractions at the back of the guide. This includes companies that undertake specialist mining trips with fully qualified leaders for those wanting to learn more about the internal workings of a mine. Not only are they qualified the leaders have a great deal of experience and knowledge about mining history.

View of slate mill with snow on mountains behind Ynysypandy Slate Mill (also known as Gorseddau or Ynysypandy Slate Factory)

Some of the pictures were taken with permission from farmers or landowners. As such these features are found on private land. Where this is the case I have indicated so. The best and most useful maps to use are the 1:25,000 Ordnance Survey Outdoor Leisure series. These are: OL 17 Snowdon/Yr Wyddfa; OL 18 Harlech, Porthmadog & Bala/Y Bala and OL 23 Cadair Idris & Llyn Tegid.

The book is divided into sections grouping quarries and mines into localised areas a sfollows:

1 – Bethesda and Llanberis
2 – Nantlle and Tal-y-sarn
3 – Cwm Pennant and Cwmystradllyn
4 – West of Blaenau Ffestiniog
5 – East of Blaenau Ffestiniog
6 – Cwm Penmachno
7 – Dinas Mawddwy and Abergynolwyn
8 – Corris and Aberllefenni

There are proposals that the 7 main slate areas of north Wales become a UNESCO World Heritage area. These are:

1. Ogwen Valley
2. Dinorwig
3. Nantlle
4. Cwmystradllyn and Cwm Pennant
5. Blaenau Ffestiniog, the Dwyryd and the Ffestiniog Railway
6. Bryneglwys, Abergynolwyn and the Talyllyn Railway
7. Aberllefenni

1. Aerial view of Dinorwig slate quarry Llanberis; 2. Llyn Padarn slate railway

The key aims of the nomination are:
1. Heritage led regeneration
2. Conservation
3. Economic development
4. Community and skills development
5. Re-connecting communities with heritage
6. Promote and celebrate the important global role of the Welsh slate industry
7. Unified story

It is hoped that UNESCO recognition and inscription will take place in July 2020.

Finally, I recommend a visit to the National Slate Museum to appreciate the plethora of quarrying and mining artefacts exhibited there as well as being able to watch a demonstration on how roofing slates are split from blocks of slate in one of the workshops. Certainly a good bet on a wet day.

Under the leadership of Gwynedd County Council the nomination has been put together with key partners. The proposal has taken into consideration the variety of technology, organisation, social and environmental impacts of the slate industry in the mountain landscapes on north Wales which once dominated world production.

1. & 2. National Slate Museum at Llanberis

What is Slate? Its formation and uses

Slate is a metamorphic rock. This means it has been altered from its original sedimentary composition. The word slate stems from the old English *slat* or perhaps even *sclat* and the French word meaning 'to split', *escalater*. The formation of slate in Snowdonia began around 500 million years ago, or Cambrian period for the Dinorwig, Penrhyn and Nantlle areas and around 450 million years ago, or Ordovician period, for Abergynolwyn, Aberllefenni, Corris and Ffestiniog slate. Originally depositions of fine sediments of clay minerals flaky in character formed a mudstone. Minerals in this determined the colour the slate was eventually to become. Depositions continued over several million years and huge pressures turned the mudstone into shale.

Continued pressure and great heat caused a chemical change to occur. The original clay minerals broke down to become other minerals such as mica and feldspar, the main constituents of this reformed and different rock, slate. Interestingly the minerals had reformed at an angle to the bedding planes. This was the line of cleavage. Some mines, notably in Gaewern a part of the Braich Goch mine complex above Corris have pure white calcite formations such as curtains, stalactites and stalagmites normally only seen in caves.

The slate above Bethesda and Nantlle tends to have a reddish purple tinge to it, whilst around Blaenau Ffestiniog and Corris it is blue grey and is much finer grained. Generally it is slate from the Cambrian period that provides the most durable and hardest slate. In fact roofing slate from the quarries in Snowdonia were regarded as the finest and most durable in the whole world withstanding the effects of extreme weather, was unaffected by frost and totally impervious to water. Combined with the cheap cost of production until the 1930's, slate was the most popular roofing material.

The Blaenau Ffestiniog vein was called the Old Vein and provided excellent roofing slate whist the Corris was named the

Finished slates at the National Museum

Narrow Vein and provided excellent slab. Another slate, found outside of Snowdonia and this guide, was formed in the Silurian period, around 430 million years ago. This is the least durable of the types but it provided good slab for indoor use.

Nowadays slate is used for a plethora of tourist souvenirs but in the past there have been many other uses. The best snooker tables had slate beds. Apart from roofing slate other uses included building material, walling, slate plank fencing, flooring, sills, lintels, quoins. It was used to form vats in both the chemical and brewing industries on account of its impervious nature. Cisterns, sold as 'flat packs', were manufactured. In farming it was used in pig sties and cowsheds, dairies and larders not to mention the Victorian 'privy' or Gents toilets. It was also used for making coffins, some of which were re-usable (probably for pauper burials) and gravestones. Slate was also used in the electricity trade where it was used for switchboards and insulation. Interestingly slate is also used in the fashion industry for making lipstick and the production of soap.

1. Slate waste used for building;
2. A slate roof on a house on the outskirts of Penygroes

Below is a list of traditional slate sizes. I have included this for amusement and it can be seen that their names are predominantly 'female'. Sizes are in inches.

Empress 26 x 16
Princess 24 x 14
Duchess 24 x 12
Small Duchess 22 x 12
Marchioness 22 x 11
Broad Countess 20 x 12
Countess 20 x 10
Small Countess 18 x 10
Viscountess 18 x 9
Wide Lady 16 x 10
Broad Lady 16 x 9
Lady 16 x 8
Small Lady 14 x 8
Narrow Lady 14 x 7
Double 12 x 6
Single 10 x 5

Many other sizes and names existed with over 30 being known at the end of the 19th century. 'Queens' could have been anything from 30 x 18 to 36 x 26 or even larger. 'Princesses' were often termed 'Fourteens'. 'Putts' were 14 x 12 sometimes called 'Headers' and 'Ladies Putts' were 13 x 10, 'Damp Course' slates came in many sizes from 20 x 9 down to 9 x 4½.

The output of roofing slate from Gwynedd slate quarries was enough to roof 14 million terraced houses.

The longest industrial dispute in British industrial history was at Penrhyn Quarry just outside Bethesda which lasted for three years starting on the 22nd November 1900. Unfortunately it heralded the demise of the reliability of slate production and orders fell sharply with thousands of workers laid off.

Aerial view of Aberllefenni slate quarry near Corris

Methods of Extracting Slate

Slate is visually extracted by one of three methods. The first is '*Hillside Working*'. Here it is either face working where the slate is dug into the hillside to form a single or several levels. If the slate is of good quality and appears to be a continuous large vein it often becomes a quarry and is then extracted from multiple galleries or terraces. The second method is '*Pit Working*'. Here a slate vein is followed down with adits or levels being driven to make life easier for transportation of the raw product. Finally there is '*Underground Working*'. This occurs when there would be too much surface material to be removed. The vein is accessed by driving adits or levels. Work would then commence along the top of the vein by driving what is known as a roofing shaft. From this progress would then be downward and across to form a chamber. A typical size would be around 22 metres wide. Another chamber would then be started leaving an intervening pillar some 13 metres wide that acted as a support for the roof. Many chambers could be developed in any mine by this process.

With today's modern mining techniques a fourth method called '*untopping*' is used to remove the surface of the ground above the vein and rob the pillars as these would be good quality slate. In its most simple form slate was extracted by attacking the slate exposure by basic and simple means such as levering and cutting out usable blocks. The tools used for this were a big oak mallet called, in Welsh, a '*Rhys*'. '*Plug and Feathers*' were also used and are wedges that expanded the rock when driven into cracks.

As these workings expanded it became evident that more rock was needed so blasting took place. Initially this was black powder. Prior to mechanisation a shot hole was drilled by the use of a '*Jumpah*', a long weighted iron rod. This was a very laborious slow method. After 1880 or so compressed air drills were used, much quicker but incredibly noisy. Eventually high explosives were used but this tended

Aerial view of Dinorwig slate quarry, looking over Llyn Padarn and Llanberis towards Caernarfon Bay

to shatter the rock. Only 10% of the rock extracted was usable. The usable blocks going to be used for roofing slates were then split using a chisel to a suitable thickness before being dressed to the required size. They were then held over a fixed blade, the '*Drafal*' and trimmed by the use of a tool similar to a knife, '*Cyllell*'.

Further developments took place with the advent of water power in the early 19th century. Circular saws developed and in the mid-20th century diamond tipped saws came into use and are now universal. They are huge things having blades two metres in diameter and even slightly larger. Instead of the coarse cut of the water powered saws these saws have a very fine cut and use water for cooling the blade. Having seen these work it is absolutely amazing to see a three ton block of slate over 300mm thick and 1.5 metres long sliced just as a knife goes through butter. Mechanical dressing developed around the same time as circular saws and was operated by hand or foot. However, splitting the slate still remains a manual process. Many attempts to mechanise this process failed.

Aerial view of Moel Tryfan slate quarry near Rhosgadfan

VIVIAN

Map: Ordnance Survey 1:25,000
Explorer OL 17 Snowdon/Yr Wyddfa
Grid reference: SH 586605.

The huge gash is easily seen from the Llanberis station of the Llanberis Lake Railway. Although classed as a separate quarry it shared all the resources of Dinorwig! Vivian was worked on 8 levels although only 6 are now visible with the other two below water. Often these levels were called 'galleries' or terraces which are spaced at a height of 18 – 22 metres. The bottom gallery was opened in 1873. The quarry closed in 1958.

About a third of the way up on the right is a fine piece of clean rock. It is on this that one of the finest slate rock climbs in the Llanberis area can be found and is named 'Comes the Dervish'. There are other climbs here and climbers can often be seen. A fine example of a 'Blondin' can be seen suspended over the pool which is used nowadays by the Vivian Diving School allowing divers to explore the 18 metres deep pool in which there are the remains of buildings and vehicles.

A notable feature is the restored V2 table incline. Wagons were transported on wedge shaped transporters that travelled on wider gauge rails. It was constructed between 1873 and 1877.

There is a public path into the quarry from the fee paying car park at Gilfach Ddu to a viewing platform overlooking the pool. It passes through a fine arch to the right of the dive centre beyond the railway line. It is also possible to walk up the right hand side of the quarry boundary to where a path goes across the top of it and down the left hand side.

1. Vivian Quarry Pool and Blondin;
2. Blondin spanning the quarry pool

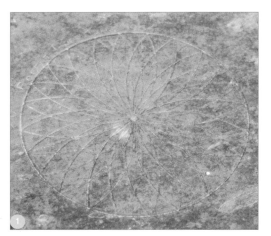

1. Slate carving on wall above Vivian quarry;
2. Detail of drum; 3. The higher drum house
Overleaf: Aerial view of workings at
Dinorwig slate quarry and Dinorwig Power
Station on shore of Llyn Peris

DINORWIG

Map: Ordnance Survey 1:25,000
Explorer OL 17 Snowdon/Yr Wyddfa
Grid reference: SH 595603.

Looking across towards Elidir Fawr this is the huge and very obvious quarry on the mountain side. Looking from the village or along the road going towards Nant Peris it appears vast. However, when walking through it the sense of awe is overcoming as it is very much bigger than casual appearances suggest.

Dinorwig Quarry is an amalgamation of many quarries and scratchings. Some of these were named after individuals such as Cloddfa Griffith Ellis, Hafod Owen, Harriet, Millington, Morgan's, Turner and Wellington. Was Turner named after the famous painter who frequented the area and was Wellington named after the Duke who routed the French at Waterloo? Who knows! Other workings under the Dinorwig banner were Alltwen, Braich (south eastern side of the quarry), Brynglas, Bryn Llys, Chwarel Mynydd, Clogwyn y Gigfran, Diffwys, Garret (north western side of the quarry), Muriau and Sofia.

Assheton-Smith the landowner started slate quarrying here in 1787. By the turn of the century there were 13 levels some 18 – 22 metres high. The first incline was built in 1789 but sledges were more often used until 1816. One of the features of Dinorwig Quarry are the 2 main inclines. These had many sections or pitches. Each pitch would connect 2 or perhaps 3 terraces. Steam locomotives arrived in the 1870's with petrol ones arriving in 1930. There were perhaps 50 miles of railway lines and 15 miles of compressed air pipes. The main mill, almost on a level with Dinorwig village, is best seen when walking back from the viewpoint. 'Blondins' were installed in the 1930's. Electric power had been used since 1905 which came from the power station in Cwm Dyli. The quarry's output in the late 1890's from around 3,000 workers was 100,000 tons per annum. When you think that would have produced over a million tons of waste to be scattered over the mountain side! That was for one year alone so how many tons of waste now lay scattered around the hillside? Work stopped in 1969.

Slate was initially sent by boat to the end of Llyn Padarn and thence to the coast by cart. The port of Port Dinorwig (Y

and ran to the head of an incline above Port Dinorwig but closed in 1962. A branch line at Port Dinorwig was opened in 1852 that gave access to the main line.

Looking at Dinorwig today one cannot imagine the extremely hazardous nature of quarrying slate. Between 1822 and 1878 there were 234 fatalities. This includes six instances when the rope securing the quarryman, broke; fifty five from rock falls; forty two from premature blasting; thirty one from falling from the edge of a gallery (or terrace) and six were drowned when the boat taking them to work across Llyn Padarn capsized in a sudden storm. Even a visitor was killed by a rock fall. This compares to the 312 who died in Penrhyn in the same period. The man who was the most vulnerable would have been the one drilling shot holes ready for the explosive. He would only have a rope wrapped around his thigh a couple of times as his sole security.

Felinheli) was constructed in 1793. Shortly afterwards a road was built thus avoiding the shipping along the lake. Things became easier in 1824 when the Dinorwig Railway came into being but ran at an unacceptable height until 1842 when the quarry at Fachwen was bought. This made things much easier allowing the Padarn Railway of 4 feet gauge to be laid alongside the lake. The line had virtually no gradient

The walled path leading down to Gilfach Ddu

1. One of many inclines in the quarry;
2. Incline leading up to the quarryman's path across the upper part of the quarry;
3. Anglesey Barracks

Snowdonia Slate

To find out more about the quarry the National Slate Museum is a must see attraction. See the appendix at the back of the book for details.

There is a very scenic public path/track through the middle part of the quarry. From the west this is accessible from the free car park at Deiniolen where the busses turn or from a large layby close to Nant Peris

1. The quarryman's path across the upper part of the quarry; 2. Quarry walls and remains of dual drum house; 3. Quarry view with the main walking path through this in lower third of the picture

Although rock climbers are tolerated there is no right of access into this quarry other than the access path/track through it.

1. The upper path across the upper half of the quarry; 2. and 3. The memorial to the quarrymen at the bus turnaround close to the massive spoil heaps at Dinorwig

1. Remains of one of the 36 saws;
2. A 'table'

1. *Ruins near the top of the Braich side of the quarry;*
2. *Typical configuration of gallery or terrace working;*
3. *Pyramid used as the anchor for a 'Blondin'*

Overleaf: One of the main inclines at Dinorwig Quarry

38	*Snowdonia Slate*

1. A typical railway point switching lever;
2. Drum house with Moel Eilio in the background;
3. Works with Llanberis far below;
4. Work area in Dinorwig;
5. Works with Llyn Peris below

Section 2 – Nantlle and Tal-y-sarn

DOROTHEA

Map: Ordnance Survey 1:25,000
Explorer OL 17 Snowdon/Yr Wyddfa
Grid reference: SH 501532.

Dorothea Quarry opened in 1820 and very quickly became the dominant undertaking in the area. Initially it was named Cloddfa Turner but renamed Dorothea after Richard Garnon's wife who owned the land at that time. The main force for quarrying around Dyffryn Nantlle (Nantlle valley) was William Turner 1776 – 1859. In 1848 records show that 200 men produced 5,000 tons per annum. Production peaked in 1872 when 17,442 tons were produced. In 1882 some 533 men were employed when production was 16,598 tons per annum. In 1891 the last pit to be opened increased the total to six. Even as late as 1930 there were still 350 men employed. As the pits deepened wire inclines were installed in the 1840's to lift the slate out. Eventually there were eight. During 1900 'Blondins' were constructed. They were originally steam powered and then by electricity from 1957.

The quarry pool is over 150 metres deep and is used as a diving venue. Many of the inclines can still be seen. There are two magnificent large slate structures known as pyramids. These were constructed to form bases for the chain inclines and also allowed spoil to be tipped behind them. The inverted arch retaining buttress featured in the photographs here is on the line of the 'Nantlle Railway'.

Flooding became a huge problem for Dorothea. In 1884 several workers were drowned when the pits was flooded by the Afon Llyfni. As such the river was realigned and the bed deepened allowing it to flow to the south of the workings as can be seen by the straight line from the road bridge on the B4418 spanning the river close to Tal-y-sarn. This only partially cured the problem, though. As the pit deepened further and further it was decided to install a Cornish Beam Engine to pump water out of it in 1904. This was replaced by electric pumps in 1951.

Lake at Tal-y-sarn slate quarry and incline and Cornish Beam Engine House at Dorothea Slate Quarry, Dyffryn Nantlle

In 1828 the Nantlle Railway enabled the quarries in the valley to have access to a port. It had a gauge of 3ft 6ins (1,067mm). Initially horse powered it ran to Caernarfon but in 1872 it went only as far as Tal-y-sarn which by then had been connected to the national British Railways network. The Nantlle Railway continued as part of British Railways until 1963 and horses still worked the line until a couple of years prior to closure. The names of the last two horses were 'Prince' and 'Corwen'. Dorothea used the line for transporting its slate from 1829 to 1959. Internal tramway systems used 2ft (610mm) gauge and was among the first users of De Winton engines in 1869.

Production dropped dramatically after the Second World War and final closure came in 1970.

Access is via the public path around the quarry pool starting either at Nantlle or Tal-y-sarn. The advantage of starting at Tal-y-sarn is it is easy to visit the quarry rim of Tal-y-sarn Quarry to view the large quarry pool on the way to Dorothea. It also gives a view, from the track, of the ruins of Tal-y-sarn Hall.

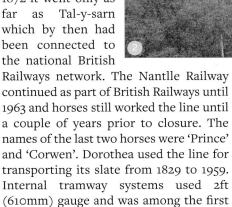

1. Dorothea Incline;
2. The old pump house at Dorothea
Overleaf: Lake at Dorothea Slate Quarry,
Dyffryn Nantlle, near Tal-y-sarn

PEN YR ORSEDD

Map: Ordnance Survey 1:25,000
Explorer OL 17 Snowdon/Yr Wyddfa
Grid reference: SH 509539

1. One of the railway line tunnels below the incline. The line led to the Nantlle Railway; 2. The left hand incline pyramid showing the cantilevered staircase; 3. One of the tramway bridges; all at Dorothea

Another large quarry, Pen yr Orsedd commenced work in 1816 obtaining its first mill in 1860. Being higher up the hill than Dorothea the quarry pit was able to be drained. The quarry developed quickly and by 1898 there were four mills on three levels. 10,000 tons of slate were produced in 1864. The workforce in 1882 was some 230 who produced 8,210 tons. This quarry was notable for the six 'Blondins' it used. They were initially steam powered. The quarry was a founder subscriber of the Cwm Dyli Power Station and they all became electrically powered and remained in use until the 1970's when access was by a newly constructed road. Unfortunately only one of the 'Blondins' remains standing today with some of the others lying forlornly on the ground.

In 1862 Pen yr Orsedd was connected to the Nantlle Railway with 3ft 6ins (1,067mm) gauge track being used on

1. Old staircase going up to upper level at Pen yr Orsedd; 2. Inverted arches above the tramway at Dorothea

every quarry level apart from the highest. Levels also had tramways with 2ft (610mm) gauge track.

The quarry closed in 1979 and was the last to close in the valley.

There is NO right of access although locals use the quarry roads to walk from Fron to Nantlle.

1. *Ruins of the works on the middle level;*
2. *'Blondin' on upper level;*
3. *Ruins of the upper level;*
4. *Winding gear in drum house powered by electricity;*
5. *Directionally aligned pulleys*

Overleaf: General view of Tal-y-sarn and Dorothea Slate Quarries, Dyffryn Nantlle, near Tal-y-sarn

Section 3 – Cwm Pennant and Cwmystradllyn

PRINCE OF WALES

Map: Ordnance Survey 1:25,000
Explorer OL 17 Snowdon/Yr Wyddfa
Grid reference: SH 549500.

This quarry situated at the head of Cwm Pennant is dominated by the Nantlle Ridge over to the left whilst the vegetated, brooding sombre cliffs of Moel Lefn soar up to the right close by. A long incline in between the spoil heaps links the five levels. Below the main workings is the reservoir that supplied water for powering the mill 37 metres lower and 350 metres away at the terminus of the Gorseddau Junction and Porthmadog Railway. The gauge of the track was 2ft (610mm) and built in 1872 to replace the 3ft (914mm) Gorseddau Tramway.

The mill only processed slate slab whilst roofing slates were fashioned on the levels. The mill is adorned with some wonderful arched doorways. Close to the mill are the remains of the launder pillars. Like Gorseddau the quarry was a terrible failure having opened in 1873 although a small development had commenced in the 1860's. The quarry closed in 1886 with sporadic working continuing until 1920. At the zenith of production around 5,000 tons were produced with a workforce of around 200.

For such an unsuccessful venture the site is well worth a visit with many substantial remains. There are five levels with building remains on all levels but the highlight is the fine series of waliau on level five. These are opposite the barracks so the men did not have far to go for their work! The barracks did not have family accommodation. Directly behind the reservoir, itself is an interesting feature in that it has a double wall with a gap in the middle, are the remains of a workshop. The gap in the dam wall would have been filled with clay and the construction

> 1. *One of the fine arches at the slate mill;*
> 2. *Two of the launder pillars by the mill with the Gorseddau Tramway beyond;*
> 3. *Tram road and inclines showing 'textbook galleries'; 4. Waliau and sheds;*
> 5. *Waliau; 6. The barracks*

allowed for the dam to be raised when required.

Access is via a right of way from the car parking area at the end of the road in Cwm Pennant although a small fee is payable at the last farm. DO NOT enter any of the adits.

Waliau in close proximity to the barracks Prince of Wales quarry

Snowdonia Slate

GORSEDDAU

Map: Ordnance Survey 1:25,000 Explorer OL 18 Harlech, Porthmadog & Bala/Y Bala Grid reference: SH 571453.

This, like Prince of Wales quarry, failed dismally. There was an enormous infrastructure associated with it, not least the Gorseddau Tramway. A huge and spectacular three storey mill was built at Ynysypandy to process slab, the main product, from the quarry.

The first scratchings started in 1807 and offered for sale in 1836. After many owners the lease was bought by a Bavarian mining engineer going by the grand name of Henry Tobias Tschudy von Uster! He maintained his interest here during the lifetime of the quarry although the lease was bought again in 1854 by Robert Gill and John Harris. These two were the prime movers in the development of the quarry. Between 1855 and 1857 £50,000, an inordinate amount of money for the day, was spent on their project.

They started making the galleries, built Plas Llyn the managers house, now a heap of rubble in the coppice on the way to the quarry and a village for the quarry workers.

They built the magnificent three storey mill at Ynysypandy for processing slab along with Evan Jones of Garndolbenmaen. The whole complex was connected to the port at Porthmadog by the Gorseddau Tramway. What little roofing slate was made was done at the quarry. Quality was poor. In 1857 only 226 tons was produced. Production peaked in 1860 at 2,148 tons and this with a workforce of 200. Production dropped steadily with only 865 tons in 1865 and a miserly 25 tons in 1867. Because of this the company folded in 1871.

Access to the quarry is by a gentle rising track, the course of the Gorseddau

1. View of Gorseddau Quarry; 2. The overhanging retaining wall at Gorseddau with Moel Hebog in the background

Tramway. There is a car park at the head of the valley and the track starts at Tyddyn Mawr where there is also a tea room.

YNYSYPANDY SLATE MILL

Map: Ordnance Survey 1:25,000 Explorer OL 18 Harlech, Porthmadog & Bala/Y Bala
Grid reference: SH 549433

This mill is of unique design. Normally a mill would be a long single storey building to facilitate easy manoeuvring of heavy slate slabs. Slab here was processed vertically through the mill! No expense was spared in setting up the machine room which ultimately had expensive saws, planers and dressing machinery. It would have seemed sensible for the slate to enter along the upper and middle tramways and to leave by the lower one but no records appear to be available as to the exact process. Inside the mill is a large gash that accommodated the 26ft (8m) overshot waterwheel. The mill specialised in the

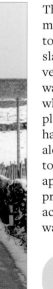

1. *The Ynysypandy slate mill*; 2. *Looking along the road towards Ynysypandy slate mill*

manufacture of items such as flooring slabs, dairies, troughs and urinals. After the failure of the quarry the mill fell into disuse although some use may have occurred with slate from Prince of Wales quarry in 1875. Local tradition reports that the mill was used a chapel whilst in 1888 an Eisteddfod was held here. In 1890 the wood floor was lifted and in 1906 the roof and iron framed windows were also taken away. The ruin toady is a Scheduled Ancient Monument.

Access is easy from directly below by a short but steep path zigzagging up to the mill.

TREFORYS VILLAGE

Long deserted there were, at one time, 36 houses here on three 'streets'. The village was named after Robert Morris Griffiths from Bangor. Built in 1857 each of the 36 houses also had a quarter of an acre of land. This was and still is poor quality and it would not have been easy to grow anything in the acidic ground. In the 1861 census 9 families were recorded as living in the village, 18 adults and 27 children, whilst in the 1871 census the village was

recorded as unoccupied. Plas Llyn, however, was still lived in but this was abandoned in 1878. At the start of the 20th century it was converted into a fishing lodge and for several years after 1949 it became a Youth Hostel but now sadly it is a just a heap of stone in the coppice below the village.

From Tyddyn Mawr follow the tramway for a little under ½ mile then turn up to the left on a right of way to the village.

1. The middle one of the three side roads in Treforys and Gorseddau Quarry; 2. The highest situated road of Treforys; 3. Ruined house and the spoil heap of Gorseddau Quarry beyond; 4. Ruins on the 'middle' street. Overleaf: Aerial overview of Dyffryn Nantlle slate quarrying area, looking north west towards Caernarfon Bay

CROESOR

Map: Ordnance Survey 1:25,000
Explorer OL 17 Snowdon/Yr Wyddfa
Grid reference: SH 657456

One of the more well-known mines in Snowdonia it is unusual in that it has no significant surface workings. There are no large spoil heaps on the surface either as most of it was put into underground chambers. The mine had mixed fortunes with work beginning in the 1840's. By 1861 two companies were working the mine. They amalgamated in 1865. This was a year after it was connected to the newly opened Croesor Tramway. At that time production was small with only 226 tons produced in 1868. The mine closed around 1880 although there was a change of owner in 1875.

Opening again in 1895 under the direction of Moses Kellow production increased with annual tonnages between 5,000 and 6,000 tons declining steadily as the market for slate fell until closure in 1930. Moses was inventive and unafraid of trying anything to improve the lot of the miner. His innovative skills allowed for many changes. Perhaps his greatest invention was the drill named after him, the Kellow drill. This was a hydraulic one and between 1898 and 1915 he obtained no fewer than 5 patents. It was a remarkable improvement that allowed a 7.5ft (2.3m) shot hole to be drilled in less than 2 minutes instead of all day using a jwmpah. The mine was ventilated by a Guibal fan and was housed close to the entrance and part of the fan housing can still be seen today.

Guibal fans or centrifugal fans had been known since 1556 but the Guibal Fan for ventilating mines was a very important one. It was patented in Belgium in 1862 by the French engineer Theophile Guibal. They have a spiral case surrounding the fan blades as well as a flexible shutter which controls the escape velocity. The fan

1. The almost flattened remains of Croesor mine; 2. The incline coming down to join the Croesor Tramway; 3. Remains of the drum house above the long incline; 4. The incline wall; 5. Remains of the housing for the Guibal Fan; 6. The Croesor Mill

The Barracks

allowed mines to be operated at great depth.

Kellow introduced electricity to the mine by generating his own at Blaencwm on the valley floor. The mine was lit by 2,000 candle power arc lights. Water came from Llyn-cwm-y-foel some 260 metres higher and two other lakes to drive the turbines. He also introduced irreversible winches and he was the first to use an electric locomotive inside the mine with the electricity coming from overhead power lines.

Usually and traditionally Welsh slate mines were worked in teams of four, consisting of two rock men who worked in the chambers below ground and two mill men who processed the slate blocks.

Kellow introduced a new system whereby the two rock men supplied the slate slabs to the mill where independent two man teams worked and allocated slabs by ballot. This enabled the mill to work at full capacity for much of the time and increased productivity by as much as 25% in the first month of operation. Although resisted at first by the work force it was quickly accepted as their wages rose!

Croesor Mine and its surface remains are easily reached from Croesor by going up gradually and across the hill on the south-east side of Cwm Croesor on a wide track. However, the mine is at a height of 477 metres and weather can and often does change. If visiting please dress accordingly. For the intrepid it is possible to do what is known as 'The Last Great Adventure'. This is an underground journey from Croesor through to Rhosydd. It is **IMPORTANT** that you go with someone who knows the mine as it is definitely not for the faint hearted as there are still many dangers. Many rope manoeuvres are needed to overcome numerous obstacles so ensure you have the necessary specialist skills to overcome these.

RHOSYDD

Map: Ordnance Survey 1:25,000
Explorer OL 17 Snowdon/Yr Wyddfa
Grid reference: SH 664461

The mine commenced extracting slate in the early 1830's and was surface worked until the 1850's when it began developing underground. It is in a remote area which made it extremely difficult to transport slate to the port. It would have been ideal to transport slate via Cwmorthin to the Ffestiniog Railway but the owners of Cwmorthin quarry objected. As a result Rhosydd slate was transported on the Croesor tramway to which the quarry became connected. This is perhaps the longest single pitch incline in Wales. Due to the huge amount of money spent on development work and poor returns the owners went bust in 1873. When quarrying first commenced the finished slates were originally transported by pack horse. A well-constructed path passed below Moelwyn Mawr with it to the west and Llyn Stwlan to the east. It then turned westward to go over the col below Moelwyn Bach and descended Cwm Maesgwm to reach the Aberglaslyn to Maentwrog turnpike road.

A new company, the New Rhosydd Sate Company Ltd bought the mine in 1874 at an auction for the paltry sum of £29,500 after it was claimed that the development work had cost £150,000. The workforce then became predominantly Welsh. For a short period the mine became quite profitable but in 1900 a large collapse occurred in the underground workings. At the start of the First World War the quarry was deemed to be non-essential and was closed. It re-opened in 1919 and was bought by the Colman family of mustard fame. They kept the mine working until 1930 when it closed. In 1947 the mine was sold again but it did not commence work and in 1948 the majority of the machinery was taken away by scrap metal men.

In 1883 the quarry was one of the largest underground quarries in Wales outside of the environs of Blaenau Ffestiniog. That year it produced 5,616 tons of slate and peaked in 1885 at 6,484 tons. At that time 207 men worked there. In total during the productive life of the mine it produced around 22,000 tons of slate. The spoil heaps have about 2.5 million tons of waste material. Amongst many other roofing projects the slates from Rhosydd roofed the Royal Mint,

1. *Surface ruins and inclines; 2. Looking down to the ruins of the upper works; 3. Upper ruins and Moelwyn Mawr; 4. Upper ruins and Cnicht; 5. Retaining wall of tip*

Chatham Dockyard, buildings on the Blenheim estate, Morris Motors' Oxford car plant and a bus garage in Barking!

Oddly the Rhosydd Mine Managers house was in Cwmorthin and titled Plas Cwmorthin. It was built in 1860 and the shell can be seen today, sheltered by a small coppice, to the right of the track when walking towards Rhosydd. On the opposite side of the track is Rhosydd Terrace just before the track rises. This was built in 1865 and by 1881 there were 41 people living there but with number 6 not listed. Amazingly 13 people lived in number 1, John Williams and his wife Elizabeth, their 6 sons and 3 daughters plus 2 lodgers! Just before the terrace is Rhosydd Stables that were used by the ponies and constructed around the same time as the terrace.

Before reaching these there is the remains of the Calvinistic Capel y Gorlan. Unfortunately the slate roof was robbed by thieves in the 1970's. It was built in 1867 and had room inside for over 100 worshippers. It closed in the 1930's.

The exploration of the surface remains of Rhosydd can be accessed from Cwmorthin by following a good track. Like Croesor, Rhosydd is situated high in the mountains with the highest workings at 577 metres. As such weather is often much different to the valley. DO NOT enter any of the levels. They are loose and dangerous and slate has a nasty habit of just falling! As mentioned previously Rhosydd can be explored but ONLY with an experienced guide and is part of what has become known as 'The Last Great Adventure' It is **IMPORTANT** that you go with someone who knows the mine because it is definitely not for the faint hearted as there are still many dangers and you have the necessary skills to overcome the many obstacles.

CWMORTHIN

Map: Ordnance Survey 1:25,000
Explorer OL 17 Snowdon/Yr Wyddfa
Grid reference: SH 680461

Spasmodic open quarry working commenced here in 1810 at the start of a long and complex history. When the 1ft 11½ins (597mm) mine tramway was connected to the Ffestiniog Railway in the early 1860's underground development started in earnest. Several different

companies ran the mine in the late 1800's with the earliest starting with 'Lake Level' by the Cwmorthin Slate Company Ltd. Development rapidly spread upwards on eight levels. Poor working practises and

1. & 2. *Cwmorthin Terrace*; 3. *Gorlan Chapel*; 4. *Cwmorthin House ruins*; 5. *Office ruin close to the mine entrance*; 6. *The entrance into Cwmorthin Mine*

water for Holland's workings, was drained as a result. Production in 1862 was only around 350 tons but in 1876 this had risen dramatically to 12,500 tons. In all around 96,000 tons of slates left the mine between 1861 and 1876.

A different company took the mine over, The New Welsh Slate Company, having just been evicted from Oakeley. They operated from Lake Level but closed off the dangerously loose upper levels. Instead they went deeper sinking 5 levels before they too closed in 1900 due to financial problems. Coming up for sale once again it was bought by Oakeley Quarry. At first they did not do any work on the lower floors and they filled with water right up to Lake Level hundreds of feet deep! It remained so until the 1930's. Oakeley were by then mining under the old Cwmorthin workings and were somewhat unhappy with all that water above them so decided it was time to drain it. Special diamond drills cut boreholes into the deepest parts of Cwmorthin from the Oakeley end. The water was then drained out under control.

Once the water had gone the two mines were connected in several places.

rash engineering lead to a severe collapse in 1884 causing the demise of that company in 1888. The ground above the collapse fractured all the way up to Allt Fawr where Llyn Bach, which provided

Cwmorthin operated as a district of Oakeley until 1970 when Oakeley closed unable to fund the cost of the pumping. This marked the end of its working life as a major concern. Ownership of both Oakeley and Cwmorthin once again split. Through the 1980's and 1990's Cwmorthin was worked by a small team of local men. Final closure came in 1997.

The mine had gained a dreadful reputation and was nicknamed 'The Slaughterhouse' due to its dire working conditions. Between 1875 and 1893 there were 21 deaths in Cwmorthin out of a workforce of some 550. In 1884 prior to the collapse around 11,600 tons of slate was produced but by 1886 this had fallen to 6,900 tons. Between 1876 and 1888 132,866 tons of slate was transported from the mine.

It is easy to explore the area as access is via the obvious wide track leading up into Cwmorthin and the lake. There is a large parking area at the end of the tarmac road just above Tanygrisiau. Immediately beyond the fine clapper bridge over the out flowing stream from the lake are the ruins of Cwmorthin Terrace or as it is known locally, Tai Llyn. The terrace was built by the owners of Cwmorthin Mine in two stages. The first eight houses were built in the 1860's from dressed stone. The other five were built more roughly in the 1870's with the 1881 census listing 13 houses. In 1871 all houses except number 7 were occupied, with 32 people living there. In 1881 all except numbers 8 and 3 were occupied. All were empty by the 1930's. Just beyond the terrace is the ruin of Capel Tiberius, an Independent Congregational chapel built at the same time as the stone cottages. It cost £100 to build and completed in 1866. Like Capel y Gorlan it could accommodate 100 worshippers.

The ruin of Cwmorthin House can be seen above the renovated white cottage. It was the home of the Agent/Quarry Manager of Cwmorthin Mine and was built in 1843. The agent at that time was Allen Searell who was quite verbose and gushing about his house. He said that it was ' a comfortable house, garden and with ground to keep a horse and cows which will make a great difference in my family in comparison with what I have been hitherto in receipt'. The house was lived in until 1943 and was the home of the last living resident of the valley.

It is possible to explore Cwmorthin

underground but, again, needs professional guidance. Check out one of the providers who use qualified and experienced guides. These companies provide specialist over-suits, helmets and lamps and other safety equipment as required.

1. On the zigzag path up to Oakeley Quarry; 2. The drum house at the top of the 1906 incline; 3. The upper incline support wall;

Overleaf: Aerial view of zig zag and incline Oakeley slate quarry Blaenau Ffestiniog; Aerial view of Oakeley slate quarry Blaenau Ffestiniog

OAKELEY

Map: Ordnance Survey 1:25,000 Explorer OL 18 Harlech, Porthmadog & Bala/Y Bala
Grid reference: SH 692465

At one time Oakeley was the largest slate quarry in Wales always excepting of course Penrhyn and Dinorwig. The quarry became an amalgamation of several workings, not least Cwmorthin! It also included the large Gloddfa Ganol, Nyth y Gigfran and Holland's with other smaller workings included. All in all it produced more than half of Blaenau Ffestiniog's total output.

The original quarry was opened in 1818 by Samuel Holland, a Liverpool merchant. It was called Rhiw at the time and on land leased near to Rhiwbryfdir Farm. The

landlords were the Oakeley family. Leased for only 3 years it was further extended by another 21 years but in 1825 sold it on to the Welsh Slate Company. It then became known as the Lower Quarry or Lord Palmerston's Quarry.

Two years later Samuel Holland opened another quarry higher up the hillside above Lower Quarry. Samuel Holland passed control over to his son also called Samuel and became known as Holland's Quarry or simply Cesail until finally settling on Upper Quarry. It was the first to send slate on the newly opened Ffestiniog Railway. In 1842 the 21 year lease expired and a new lease was signed with the Oakeley family but had to give land away from both those quarries to allow another quarry to open. Known at first as Middle Quarry it later became known as Gloddfa Ganol and operated by

1. Oakeley Quarry scene with Cribau in the back; 2. Nearing the top of the zigzag path; 3. The ruin on the right of the drum house note the pretty salte design on the roof; 4. The upper incline and shortened chimney stack; 5. The fine wall feature on the right at the top of the upper incline; 6. Ruin with Moel Penamnen beyond; 7. Upper ruins; 8. Ruin on upper level

the Rhiwbryfdir Slate Company.

In 1840 with most of the surface slate exhausted underground development took place. The lease of these three companies had clauses written in to them that forbade any intrusion into each other's workings. The 1870's saw the peak of production. The leases for the Upper and Middle Quarries expired in 1878. The landowner William Edward Oakeley refused to extend them and consolidated the two quarries into Oakeley Quarry. The Welsh Slate Company still continued to operate the Lower Quarry having negotiated a new lease some years before it expired.

The Welsh Slate Company's Lower Quarry extended directly below that of the Middle Quarry. Quarrying was taking place much more slowly in the Middle Quarry and progress became limited. As such a dangerous decision was taken to take slate from the walls of the Lower Quarry that supported the Middle Quarry workings above! Obviously rock fall became an increasing problem during the 1870's. Inevitably a huge rock fall occurred on the 6th December 1882 forcing The Welsh Slate Company to close down all workings.

The instability of the mine remained and on the 16th February 1883 in the 'Great Fall' some 6.25 million tons of rock fell all at once! This severely damaged the workings. As such a court case between Oakeley and The Welsh Slate Company was won by Oakeley and, unable to pay the hefty fine The Welsh Slate Company gave up its lease and all the workings amalgamated to become Oakeley Quarry.

The quarry closed in 1969 and liquidated in 1972.

Oakeley Quarry has NO access to the public. However, some remains can be seen by the diligent. The foot of the zigzag path can be reached and is a fine sight. To the left of it is the 1906 incline with a drum house visible at the top of it. The Nyth y Gigfran incline can also be seen quite clearly from the back road through Blaenau Ffestiniog.

WRYSGAN

Map: Ordnance Survey 1:25,000
Explorer OL 17 Snowdon/Yr Wyddfa
Grid reference: SH 677455

The extraction of slate at this underground quarry began around 1830 by William Roberts of Coed-y-Bleddiau. He subsequently sold it but the new owner lost money. Methusalem Jones tried to make it pay but again he failed losing a considerable sum of money but avoiding bankruptcy. A new group bought the mine in 1844 but due to the incline they had started to build they went bust.

Another company formed in 1850, the Wrysgan Slate and Slab Quarries Company Ltd who successfully completed the

1. Tramway to nowhere!; 2. Remains of the headgear at the top of the main incline; 3. The rusted engine; 4. Part of the belt mechanism; 5. Remains of the works on the middle level

incline started earlier. One source suggests that it went down to the Ffestiniog Railway whilst another suggests it went down into Cwmorthin which is the most likely. Before the incline was built finished slates were taken down a steep zigzagging path into Cwmorthin. A mill for processing the slate was built in 1854 and a second one in 1865 at a lower level.

The spectacular incline descending 180 metres (600 feet) down to the Ffestiniog Railway was completed in 1872. Just like the Rhosydd Incline this was a catenary. *In physics and geometry, a catenary is the curve that an idealised hanging chain or cable assumes under its own weight when supported only at its ends.* Unfortunately the foot of the incline was too shallow to be totally self-acting. As such a stationary steam engine was installed to raise the empty wagons back up to the quarry. The incline passes through a tunnel at the top and along a short cutting to the mill. The

1. Drum house at the top of incline from the works to the lower level looking towards Cwmorthin mine spoil heaps;
2. A general view of the works on the middle level beyond head of main incline;
3. View of the buildings on the middle level

incline simplified greatly the transport of slate. Most of it went to Minffordd on the gravity run line that went from Blaenau Ffestiniog to Boston Lodge. Brakes-men controlled the speed of the train. Unfortunately the gradient at Wrysgan was insufficient to re-start the gravity train after it had been loaded with slates and needed a push by a locomotive.

In Wrysgan, like most of the underground workings, slate was excavated from a series of chambers having pillars of rock between then to support the roof. Usually chambers were around 15 metres wide (50 feet) with pillars of 9 metres (30 feet). Some chambers here were exceptionally wide being up to 40 metres (130 feet) wide with only 15 metres (50 feet) of rock to support the roof.

The power source for the mills was by water wheel. Water came from the small but pretty Llyn Wrysgan. It was fed by leats and supply was often insufficient for the needs of the machinery. Around 1890 a steam engine was installed into the lower mill whilst another drove the underground incline.

Output fluctuated wildly but by 1904 it was around 3,000 tons with a workforce of over 100 men working on 8 levels. Demand for slate had started to fall as did the fortunes of Wrysgan. In the late 1930's employment fell to only 30 or so men and during the period 1945 to 1946 there were only 11 men working who produced just 348 tons a year. Final closure came in 1950.

Due to the high cost of running steam engines negotiations to use the water powered and unused Cwmorthin Cross Mill were unsuccessful. They decided to replace the steam engine with a 50hp producer gas engine to drive the mill machinery along with an external water balance being used to bring slate from the lower levels up to the mill. Interestingly, later on, the incline was powered by a car engine, the manager's Lea Francis! Electricity was installed in the early 1920's.

There is access to the surface features of this mine. A path goes up small inclines through the remains to Llyn Wrysgan. The incline tunnel can be reached from the main mill area where there are the remains of the head gear and a lorry engine! All the levels that enter the mine are loose and entry is NOT advised. There is much loose rock and there have been recent rock falls.

Section 5 – East of Blaenau Ffestiniog

BOWYDD

Map: Ordnance Survey 1:25,000 Explorer OL 18 Harlech, Porthmadog & Bala/Y Bala Grid reference: SH 708464

Work started here in the late 1760's by men coming from Cilgwyn Quarry above Tal-y-sarn in the Nantlle Valley. The original quarry has been totally obliterated. In 1870 the Votty and Bowydd Quarry amalgamated and Bowydd is now generally accepted as the name. In 1825 it was one of the first to use an internal rail system. An incline connected the quarry to the Ffestiniog Railway in 1854.

In 1882 it produced 12,100 tons of slate from a workforce of 350. Peak production came at the end of the 19th century when over 17,000 tons of slate was produced when the workforce had risen to 500. The quarry became the first one in north Wales to use electricity but output was low so water power continued to be used. Electricity was generated at Dolwen from a hydro-electric scheme. In 1930 a hydrostat was constructed to raise water when water balances were used.

As with other quarries and mines in the area the demand for slate fell sharply after World War I and in 1933 Bowydd was acquired by the owners of Oakeley Quarry. They continued to work it until 1962 when it closed going into liquidation in 1964. The workings were sold to the nearby Maenofferen Quarry and then acquired by the Greaves family the owners of Llechwedd Quarry (now a fine tourist attraction, with many and varied activities). Recently Llechwedd started un-topping to obtain slate from the underground chambers and pillars.

Bowydd is situated on private ground but there are many paths the locals use through the old workings. Access can be made from the main car park in the middle of Blaenau Ffestiniog opposite the turning down to the station for both the Conwy Valley line and the Ffestiniog Railway.

1. Incline, drum house and mill;
2. Looking down an incline to Blaenau Ffestiniog, Moelwyn Bach, Craigysgafn, Moelwyn Mawr and Moel yr Hydd;
3. Chimney and remains of boiler house;
4. The start of the walled path leading through the quarry at the end of the road just beyond Pant-yr-ynn mill

DIPHWYS or DIPHWYS CASSON sometimes DIFFWYS QUARRY

Map: Ordnance Survey 1:25,000 Explorer OL 18 Harlech, Porthmadog & Bala/Y Bala
Grid reference: SH 712463

As at Bowydd quarrying started in the late 1760's by men from Cilgwyn Quarry above Tal-y-sarn in the Nantlle Valley. They were led by Methusalem Jones who, after a dream, thought that the area was a great place to look for slate. It became the first organised quarry in the area. Unfortunately the site of the original quarry has been obscured by subsequent quarrying activities. In 1800 the quarry managers were William Turner and William Casson both of whom hailed from the Lake District By 1820 they had commenced work underground.

Between 1820 and 1880 the mine was successful but in 1890 it closed before commencing again in 1920 for another seven years scaling down production until final closure in 1955. In the 1980's Llechwedd started un-topping work. In 1820 it was the dominant quarry in the area and around 6,000 tons per annum were extracted but due to the fast and astounding growth of neighbouring quarries it was not until the 1870's that it once again regained its former position. Before connection was made to the Ffestiniog Railway a mill was built in 1845 close to town at Pant yr Ynn. The stream powering the water wheel was the Afon Bowydd. The wheel is still visible today and can be seen from the minor dead end road on the eastern side of Blaenau Ffestiniog.

In the early days of production the quarry was a pioneer in the use of saws and inclines as well as internal tramways. A reluctance to use the Ffestiniog Railway at first, it was not until 1860 that a connection was made to it via the Bowydd Incline before constructing their own in 1863.

Although, like Bowydd, the quarry is on private ground an exploration is possible by utilising the right of way from the main car park in Blaenau Ffestiniog that passes through Maenofferen Quarry.

1. Ruins of the works in Diphwys; 2. Drum house; 3. General view of the Diphwys ruins Overleaf: Aerial view of Prince of Wales quarry with Snowdon, Lliwedd and Yr Aran in the background

Snowdonia Slate

Section 6 – Cwm Penmachno

BLAEN Y CWM

Map: Ordnance Survey 1:25,000 Explorer OL 18 Harlech, Porthmadog & Bala/Y Bala
Grid reference: SH 734460

Work first started here around 1813 and continued intermittently until final closure on the 8th May 1914. Slate went down to Blaenau Ffestiniog via the Rhiwbach Tramway from 1863. Prior to that output was carted northwards down into Cwm Penmachno and thence to the quay at Trefriw. The slate would then have been loaded on to a boat to be transported down the Afon Conwy. These days it is hard to imagine boats coming up the Afon Conwy as far as Trefriw. Later the slate went via Cwm Teigl to the Afon Dwyryd and on to the dock at Porthmadog.

The 1870's saw greater development and the mill built. During the life of the mine there were many owners. At the start the land was owned by the Wynne family of Peniarth. In 1838 the quarry was leased for 21 years but unsuccessfully and the lease surrendered. In 1853 the quarry was worked again but only for two years.

In 1854 the lease was again surrendered. It was not until 1861 that a new lease was taken up. However, this was transacted shadily between different people until finally a more permanent leaseholder took over. The company that set up was known as the Blaen y Cwm Slate Company. Small scale production continued steadily and the quarry became re-named Pen-y-ffridd. In 1888 the mine was closed but opened again in 1889 but closing quickly in 1890. Production ceased again between 1891 and 1897.

The mill and wheel housing to the left

Another attempt started in 1898 under the ownership of the new Blaen y Cwm Slate Quarry Company Ltd. That too did not last long and closed in 1903 having been voluntarily wound up. In 1904 another new company worked the site until 1906. This was followed by yet another break in production until 1910 but final closure came 4 years later just before the outbreak of World War I.

The mill is a prominent and easily seen feature down to the right of the tramway when approaching from Rhiwbach.

CWT Y BUGAIL

Map: Ordnance Survey 1:25,000 Explorer OL 18 Harlech, Porthmadog & Bala/Y Bala
Grid reference: SH 733469

A close neighbour of Blaen y Cwm, quarrying commenced in the 1820's and connected to the Rhiwbach Tramway in 1863 whereupon development greatly increased. In the 1870's output was over 3,500 tons per annum from a workforce of 116 men. They lived in barracks, due to the remoteness of the site with the ruins still visible today. Interestingly one of the

barrack houses was rent free for a worker whose wife cooked for the men and cleaned the other barracks. Also visible is the ruin of the substantial mill.

There were underground workings and the retaining wall above the entrance is a fine feature. The machinery and inclines were originally steam powered but replaced by an oil engine just after World War II. As the tramway had a steep approach the loaded wagons were cable hauled up to it at first before petrol tractors were used. However, these were limited to two loaded wagons. Closing in 1961 Cwt y Bugail was the last quarry to use the Rhiwbach Tramway.

Cwt y Bugail when translated into English means 'Shepherds Hut', Cwt means hut and Bugail, shepherd. Bugail is very similar to the Gaelic, Buachaille as in the Scottish mountain Buachaille Etive Mor, 'Big Shepherd of Etive'. Rhiwbach Quarry lost its connection to the tramway in 1956 and the line lifted between it and Cwt y Bugail at that time. The line from Cwt y Bugail to Maenofferen Quarry was lifted in 1964.

Access is via the right of way from Cwm Penmachno through the workings of

Rhiwfachno and Rhiwbach to go up the incline to reach the tramway from which access is easily made beyond Blaen y Cwm.

RHIWBACH/RHIWFACHNO (CWM MACHNO)

Map: Ordnance Survey 1:25,000 Explorer OL 18 Harlech, Porthmadog & Bala/Y Bala
Grid reference: Rhiwbach SH 740462
Rhiwfachno SH 752470

Work really commenced in 1812 after the local people had been scratching around and extracting slate for their own use. Serious development took place from 1849 but transporting the slate was somewhat of a problem. Output was carted northwards down into Cwm Penmachno and thence to the quay at Trefriw. The slate would then have been loaded on to a boat to be transported down the Afon Conwy. These days it is hard to imagine

1. General view of the ruins;
2. The large entrance to Cwt y Bugail;
3. Looking down on the working area with Manod Mawr in the background

boats coming up the Afon Conwy as far as Trefriw!

However, a shorter route lay to the south by carting the product to Maentwrog down Cwm Teigl and then down the Afon Dwyryd to the port at Porthmadog. This route became favoured in the late 1830's.

Fortunately the Rhiwbach Tramway made life very much easier for getting the slate out and down to Blaenau Ffestiniog after 1863. The track gauge was 1ft 11½ins (597mm).

Being a very remote site a community developed. Houses were built along with barracks for non married workers and a schoolroom that doubled as a chapel. One of the married women kept a shop known as a 'Parlour Shop'. The main shopping was done down in Blaenau Ffestiniog on Saturdays and the goods were brought up with first empty wagons on Mondays. The school mistress also came this way on Mondays who then returned via the Graig Ddu wild car.

Output reached a peak of around 8,000 tons in 1869 but fell sharply to less than half that amount over the next few years. In 1890 there were only 81 workers

who produced the modest amount of 2,260 tons. In the 1890's the 200 metres long Glyn Aber drainage tunnel was dug. (This is the gated access used by today's mine explorers and there are companies that specialise in taking people through the mine). By 1935 output was a meagre 1,000 tons and by 1952 the mine had closed although two men still lived in a barrack on the site. They were the last to do so in the Welsh slate industry.

There is much to see on this site and certainly one of the best for remains of a past industry. A right of way starts from Cwm Penmachno and passes through the lower workings of **Rhiwfachno** (or **Cwm Machno**).

Rhiwfachno Quarry started being worked in 1818 and worked almost continuously

1. Incline remains and three launder pillars jutting above it; 2. The breached dam of the reservoir for the works at Rhiwfachno; 3. The upper works of Rhiwbach; 4. The fine boiler house chimney at Rhiwbach showing the adjacent ruins of the upper working area; 5. Tunnel through the incline at Rhiwfachno; 6. Remains of slate fence

1. *The upper mill at Rhiwbach;*
2. *View of Rhiwbach 'village' from above;*
3. *Looking down the incline to the boiler house; 4. The drum house, the incline and the mill at Rhiwbach*

until 1962. There were three mills but the area where they were has been landscaped with two small buildings and a part of a mill the only remnants. The fine crenulated wall was demolished and much of the tips were used to fill in the pit. The most obvious feature is the fine table incline. This brought block down to the mills from the upper workings whilst rubbish was up hauled. The quarry provided work for at least 100 men until the onset of World War II. It only closed because of the lack of skilled manpower. Slate was initially carted to Trefriw wharf then later to Betws-y-coed station.

Beyond Rhiwfachno the breached dam is passed and the track continues through a small forest to where, just beyond, the ruined village is seen. Higher up is a fine boiler house chimney below the incline leading up to the Rhiwbach Tramway. Although quite a long steep walk the visit to Rhiwfachno, Rhiwbach, Blaen y Cwm and Cwt y Bugail is well worth the effort.

Section 7 – Dinas Mawddwy and Abergynolwyn

MINLLYN

Map: Ordnance Survey 1:25,000
Explorer OL 23 Cadair Idris & Llyn Tegid
Grid reference: SH 852139

Work commenced here in the early 1800's with underground development commencing in the 1840's. Employment levels were high but output low. On site a mill reduced the mined slate before it was transported down an incline to the valley floor where another mill had been built. Other, much smaller, workings used this mill. The finished slate was taken on a short tramway to the Mawddwy Railway (Dinas Mawddwy). The mine closed in 1925.

Starting from Dinas Mawddwy access is from a forestry road up a steep footpath to the workings. Most notable is the fine arch under which issues a stream. Following this through the short tunnel leads to the base of the pit and the entrance into the underground workings. As with other 'open' entrances DO NOT enter unless you are with someone who knows the mine as there is deep water inside as well as areas of loose rock.

1. *Ruin of the chimney;*
2. *General view of ruins with the ruined chimney on the left*

BRYNEGLWYS

Map: Ordnance Survey 1:25,000
Explorer OL 23 Cadair Idris & Llyn Tegid
Grid reference: SH 695054

This was the largest quarry south of Blaenau Ffestiniog with workings and spoil spread over a wide area. Initially

work started as several surface scratchings in the early 1800's on farmland before being developed underground at both Cantrebedd and Bryneglwys farms in the 1840's. Due to the lack of cotton arriving from America during the Civil War and their mills idle Lancashire men came down and worked in the quarry. They also built the Talyllyn Railway which opened in 1866 and whilst not going directly to a

dock it did go to interchange on the Tywyn Cambrian Railway. Prior to this slate was taken out by packhorse to Pennal and then onto the dock at Aberdyfi. John Pugh of Penegoes, a village not far from Machynlleth, started extracting slate from Bryn Eglwys in 1844.

In 1864 it was taken over by the Aberdyfi Slate Company Ltd who built 70 houses in Abergynolwyn. As demand for roofing slates increased some 8,000 tons of these were produced in 1877. However, the cost of producing them was high and the company became unprofitable. In 1881

1. *Drum house;*
2. *Remains of the wheel pits;*
3. *The top of the New Mill shaft*

the quarry was sold to William McConnell whose family continued operations until 1911 when it was sold to Mr (later Sir) Henry Haydn Jones MP. Just prior to World War I starting production then increased to around 4,000 tons but declined after that until final closure in 1946. *An engine on the Talyllyn Railway is named after him.* The quarry never really made much profit if any at all.

Access is easy either by taking the train journey from Tywyn to Nant Gwernol or walking up from Abergynolwyn. Walking from either of these two points is on good forest roads and clearly marked paths. There are wind up radios at several points telling the story of the area. A number of ruins can be found herewith. At one point a fine waterfall plunges into a pit although a little bushwacking is required to find it!

Overleaf: Aerial overview of slate quarries and town Blaenau Ffestiniog

Section 8 – Corris and Aberllefenni

ABERLLEFENNI (FOEL GROCHAN)

Map: Ordnance Survey 1:25,000
Explorer OL 23 Cadair Idris & Llyn Tegid
Grid reference: SH 769103

The area around Aberllefenni and Corris was nicknamed 'Mini Blaenau' due to the number of quarries and mines around here some of which are quite extensive. The only featured working herein is Aberllefenni and is to the east of the road through Cwm Hen-gae. Work commenced here in the late 14th century producing top quality slate slab. Fortunately Aberllefenni was close to the road and there was little problem getting the slate out, unlike several of the other quarries in the area that were situated quite a long way from the road.

It was not until 1859 that the horse drawn and gravity tramway of the Corris, Machynlleth and River Dovey Tramway made life much easier for all. Slate was transported to the dock at Cei Ward close to Derwenlas and shipped on from there.

Derwenlas was nicknamed the 'Rotterdam of Montgomery'. (*The old county of Montgomery is now a constituent part of Powys*). This continued until the arrival of the main Cambrian Railway at Machynlleth in 1867. As such there was now no need for the tramway to go further and the section Machynlleth to Derwenlas closed. Close to the petrol station where the road goes under the railway line is the bricked up arch of the old tramway. Corris Railway closed in 1948 but today the line has been re-opened as a tourist attraction as far as Maespoeth, half a mile away, by enthusiasts who are optimistically hoping to extend the line as far as Pantperthog.

Slate, as mentioned above, was extracted mainly as slab but of the highest quality due to the lack of joints. Early working was high up the hillside of Foel Grochan and later called 'Alma'. This is a huge hole and cavern in the hillside readily seen from the road. In 1853 it was said that a slab of slate of 125 tons (approximately 5.2metres x 3 metres x 3 metres) was taken out from here. The slate vein dips at 70

1. The 'Alma' at Aberllefenni on Foel Grochan to NE of road up the valley;
2. The steps leading down from the tramway to the road at Aberllefenni;
3. A 2.2m slate saw;
4. The remains of a Rushton Crane on the east side of Aberllefenni slate mine

degrees and runs straight through Foel Grochan. In direct contrast to usual practise of upward working the workings here were downward. In 1882 a paper was written by Sir Charles Foster describes how it was done.

Basically the process involved boring eight tunnels at around 20 metres intervals and by starting at the highest level work went downward with the extracted material being dropped into the tunnel below. In 1883 over 4,800 tons of slate was produced with a workforce of 158. Just before reaching the spoil heap below the 'Alma' is the reservoir that was used to supply water to the mill. The mill is still working today and well worth a visit. Just ask before entering. To see a block of slate of several tons being cut by one of the diamond saws is mind boggling. One of the saws is 2.2 metres in diameter!

On entering the village a fine set of cantilevered steps can be seen that lead up from the road to the tramway. Aberllefenni Terrace, opposite the mill, was built and owned by the quarry owners. This was the last of the quarry tramways to operate and ran between the quarry and the mill. It closed in the 1970's.

Access is easy as much can be seen from the road. However, for the those wanting some exploration the back of the mine, in which there are the remains of a Rushton Crane, can be reached by a public footpath.

There are other quarries situated opposite Foel Grocahn and access is difficult although a footpath from the village goes along the base of the spoil heaps to reach Bluemaris. The path passes below Ceunant Ddu and Hen Gloddfa and classed as part of the Aberllefenni workings.

ABERCWMEIDDAU

Map: Ordnance Survey 1:25,000
Explorer OL 23 Cadair Idris & Llyn Tegid
Grid reference: SH 745092

Famous today because of the so called 'Corris Binocular'. Work commenced in 1849. Initially the quarried slate was brought out by being lowered on an incline and later by a level tramway worked by a locomotive. This is the track that passes above the quarry. In 1879 some 130 men worked here who produced 3,231 tons rising to 188 men in 1882 who produced 4,173 tons but plummeted in 1883 to 2,875 tons with a working force of only 80 men. As the pit deepened a tunnel was driven to drain it. Work stopped in 1905 but continued small scale extraction carried on until the 1930's.

The 'Corris Binocular' is a pair of tunnels. The right hand one is 10 metres long but the left hand one is 80 metres long. They were driven in the late 1860's possibly by a wire rope driven disc machine.

There is no right of access but the tramway starting from the back road in Upper Corris is accessible and goes across the top of the quarry. The continuation track makes for a short but good circular walk. There is a great danger of falling rock from the quarry face into the floor of the quarry which has to be gained to see the twin holes. The climb up to them is steep and loose and is not recommended.

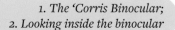
1. *The 'Corris Binocular;*
2. *Looking inside the binocular*

CHWAREL Y PENRHYN (Penrhyn Quarry)

Map: Ordnance Survey 1:25,000
Explorer OL 17 Snowdon/Yr Wyddfa
Grid reference: SH 769103

In 1781, Richard Pennant, the son of a sugar and slave baron from the Caribbean, inherited the Penrhyn estate which stretched from Bangor up the Ogwen valley to the mountain peaks. The estate was in a pretty dismal state after years of neglect. Pennant used his wealth and employed a large number of workers, more than had ever been seen in this area, to profit from the slates that were being quarried from the slopes of the valley.

As industrial towns and cities grew across the globe, there was an ever-increasing demand for roofing slates. In 1786 Pennant built a quay at the mouth of Afon Cegin in order to export slates to markets in Britain, Ireland and the rapidly developing new world. The small port was named Porth Penrhyn, and in 1801 an iron tram track was constructed from the quarry at Bethesda to the port, a revolutionary invention at the time. Lord Penrhyn, as he became known, ruled his work force with an iron hand and as a result Welsh slate became the cheapest roofing material on the market.

The amount of slates exported from Porth Penrhyn increased from 25,000 tons in 1815 to over 80,000 in 1840, reaching a climax of 135,000 tons in 1862. The quarry's railway was linked to the main Chester to Holyhead line in 1852, and in 1855 a second quay was built in the port.

The quarrymen's culture was of course totally different to that of the quarry owners. As Bethesda's name suggests, the focus of the quarrymen and their families was the Welsh Nonconformists culture of the chapel, which was completely alien to the high-anglicanism of the quarry owners. This conflict in cultures and religion reached a climax during the Great Strikes

1. Porth Penrhyn; 2. Penrhyn Castle – the seat of Lord Penrhyn, the quarry owner; 3. A great slab of Penrhyn slate

at Penrhyn quarry between 1896-97 and 1900-1903.

By that time George Sholto Douglas Pennant was Lord Penrhyn, and he was determined that the quarrymen would not have the 'right to unite', i.e. become members of the North Wales Quarrymen's Union, which was established in 1874. The quarrymen and their families suffered terribly. A few succumbed and returned to work as *'bradwyr'* ('traitors'), while others had to leave and seek work in the coal mines of southern Wales. The scars left by

1. The great slate tip of Penrhyn;
2. A slate fence near Penrhyn

the conflict can still be felt in the Bangor and Bethesda areas to this day, and despite the fact that the Penrhyn family contributed a great deal to Bangor's economic and social life, many people still feel bitter about the family's attitude towards the quarrymen and their culture.

The slate memorial at Bethesda for the Great Penrhyn Strike, 1900-1903

Appendixes

Tourist mines and other slate based attractions

NATIONAL SLATE MUSEUM

Situated on the outskirts of Llanberis close to Llyn Padarn this tells the story about a way of life. Not only is it the best place for experiencing life as it was during the slate mining days it also gives an insight into the rigours of extracting and fashioning the slate. There are regular demonstrations on how slates are split. There is operational machinery and the 15.4 metres high water wheel is the largest on the British mainland. The experience is free other than the Council operated car park. A whole day could be spent here looking at the exhibits and exploring one or more of the slate paths described earlier. For more information look at the web site: www.slate@museumwales.ac.uk or telephone 0300 111 2 333

NOTE when visiting the following show mines please be aware that the temperature inside is well below that outside in summer. It is between 8 to 10 degrees C (around 50 degrees F). As such it is advisable to wear warm clothing. Wear shoes or boots having a good grip as floors can be slippery.

LLECHWEDD SLATE CAVERNS

This is situated on the outskirts of Blaenau Ffestiniog some ¾ mile north of the town. There are many attractions here not least is the story of the Llechwedd Caverns in the interpretive centre. This also shows how slate was extracted and processed. There is also a reconstructed village showing how the miners lived. Access to the underground workings is by a funicular railway. Descending over 500 feet it is the steepest passenger railway in Britain. The tour involves visiting 10 huge chambers and ½ mile of tunnels to arrive at a very beautiful underground lake. In fact the mine has over 25 miles of tunnels. Other attractions here include mountain biking, zip lines and a huge underground trampoline. For more information look at the web site: www.llechwedd-slate-caverns.co.uk or telephone 01766 830306.

Llechwedd was first mined in 1848 and slate production was greatly improved by new technologies such as slate cutting saws in 1851. In the 1920's electricity was introduced which powered the underground railway systems. John Greaves was the owner of Llechwedd as well as several others in the area and he was much involved with the Ffestiniog Railway. This enabled slate products being transported to a private quay in Porthmadog before being shipped to the four corners of the world. Germany had a great demand for Llechwedd slate products.

There are other developments here – Bounce Below, Zip World Titan and Antur

Stiniog. This last is a not for profit organisation set up in 2007 with a view 'to develop the potential of the Outdoor Sector in the Ffestiniog area in a sustainable and innovative way for the benefit of the local residents and economy'. They have developed a series of exciting mountain bike trails in the area and are aiming to develop the disused railway line between Blaenau Ffestiniog and Trawsfynydd. A unique, to the UK, Velorail project is also planned along this. The concept uses low carbon, sustainable bicycle technology to propel an adapted carriage along the disused railway line. This would make it attractive to families.

LLANFAIR SLATE CAVERNS

Although smaller than Llechwedd Caverns it is no less impressive. Situated not far from Harlech on the A496 coast road the mine is entered down Jacobs Ladder and you are free to explore. On emerging there is a breath-taking view of Cardigan Bay, stretching all the way from the Preseli Mountains in Carmarthenshire to the Llyn Peninsula, whilst closer to is Shell Island. For more information look at the web site: www.llanfairslatecaverns.co.uk or telephone 01766 780247.

Slate was mined here between 1890 and 1910. Here there it is possible to explore the caverns by yourself. Some of the scenes of the 1995 film 'First Knight' were filmed here.

KING ARTHUR'S LABYRINTH

A part of Corris Craft Centre, close to Machynlleth, this show mine is explored by boat and foot. Themed on King Arthur it is best described as an underground storytelling adventure. A mysterious hooded boatman takes you through a magical waterfall into the world of King Arthur and the Dark Ages. Once the boat is docked the 'hooded' boatman guides you through vast caverns and tunnels telling stories about those times as well as some Welsh legends. Light and sound bring these to life. The Labyrinth is part of the Braich Goch Mine and is on level 6. For more information look at the web site: www.kingarthurslabyrinth.co.uk or telephone 01654 761584. Note that during winter months staff are often not present so delays in returning calls may be experienced.

Next to the Labyrinth there is a Stone Circle. A twisting path in the simple maze hides 8 mythical stories with some very interesting characters. Find all the clues and you win a prize!

CORRIS MINE EXPLORERS

For the adventurous Corris Mine Explorers gives people a chance to explore the ancient working of Braich Goch Mine. Although there are 7 levels the exploration covers 3 of these, levels 4, 5 and 6. There are three trips available: Taster, a 2 hour Mine Explorer and a ½ day (4 hours) Mine Expedition. Further information and bookings can be made at www.corrismineexplorers.co.uk or telephone 01654 761244.

Slate quarrying at Corris dates back to the 14th century when the Foel Grochan quarry above Aberllefenni was first mined The Braich Goch and Gaewern mines began around 1812 with Gaewern being the first of the two to be worked with Braich Goch itself starting in 1836. In 1848 working at Gaewern ceased but re-started in 1853. During its heyday some 250 men worked in the mine in 1878 and around 7,000 tons of slab and roofing slates were mined. Rising costs and demand saw the mine company collapse in 1906 although 6 companies continued work until 1970 when the mine finally closed.

ELECTRIC MOUNTAIN

Visiting the vast underground tunnels and chambers of this underground power station is an amazing experience. But why build one here? In the 1950's a pumped storage scheme was undertaken at Blaenau Ffestiniog and was highly successful. As such another scheme was planned. The ideal situation was found on Elidir Fawr. Marchlyn Mawr a small lake below the summit and in the valley Llyn Peris. The huge rambling scar of the Dinorwig quarries provided the ideal place in which to build tunnels to house the power station It took 10 years to build as well as enlarging the lakes and was opened by Prince Charles in 1984. Further information can be obtained at www.electricmountain.co.uk or telephone 01286 870636.

Quarrying first took place in 1787. Production increased after 1824 to the extent that around 100,000 tons of slate was produced. Bear in mind that for every 10 tons of rock quarried only 1 ton was usable! At its peak in the late 19th century over 3,000 men worked there and at the time it was the largest opencast slate producer in the country. By 1930 the workforce had shrunk to 2,000 and in 1969

production ceased. The slate vein is almost vertical. As such it was worked in stepped galleries.

INIGO JONES SLATE WORKS

Initially the works were established in 1861 to prefabricate school writing slates. Nowadays, self-guided tours of the works give an opportunity to have a go at calligraphy and engraving a piece of slate that you get to keep as a souvenir. There is a large showroom where its slate products are available for purchase as are other Welsh and Celtic gifts. Tours were introduced in the early 1980's by popular demand and commences with a video presentation followed by wandering through the workshops accompanied with a personal taped commentary. There is also a café opening at 10.00 to 17.00. The site is open every day of the year excepting for Christmas and Boxing Days and New Year's Day from 09.00 to 17.00 with a last tour at 16.00. Dogs are welcome. More information can be obtained at www.inigojones.co.uk or calling 01286 830242.

ZIP WORLD

Opening in March 2013 ZIP WORLD VELOCITY in Bethesda quickly achieved international fame. There are four zip lines, each a mile long, where it is possible to achieve speeds of 100 mph! The wires are 500 feet above the ground making the experience the nearest thing to human flight. The Adventure Terminal provides stunning views of Velocity, Penrhyn

Quarry and the lake. Further information can be obtained at www.zipworld.co.uk or telephone 01248 601444.

GO BELOW

For some great underground adventures and challenges this company has a big selection of trips from 5 hours to all day. The mines they explore are some of the longest and deepest in Snowdonia. Mines such as Cwmorthin above Tanygrisiau and Rhiwbach in Cwm Penmachno have a variety of trips. They have bases in Tanygrisiau close to Blaenau Ffestiniog and at Conwy Falls near to Betws y Coed. Further information and bookings can be made at www.go-below.co.uk or telephone 01690 710108.

CENTRE FOR ALTERNATIVE TECHNOLOGY (CAT)

This is situated in the old quarry of Llyngwern just off the A487 some 3 miles north of Machynlleth. There is much to discover here regarding living a greener life form what can be done to your home, how Britain can become Zero Carbon, Green Bookshop, the water balance cliff railway, information on renewable energy, mole hole and quarry trail. There is also a café.

Further information can be found at www.cat.org.uk or telephone 01654 705950 or email visit@cat.org.uk

Oakeley and Llechwedd quarries, Blaenau Ffestiniog

Slate Heritage Narrow Gauge Railways

FFESTINIOG RAILWAY

The Ffestiniog railway is located mainly within Snowdonia National Park, and the 13½ mile journey takes us from the harbour of Porthmadog to the slate town of Blaenau Ffestiniog.
www.festrail.co.uk

WELSH HIGHLAND RAILWAY

The longest heritage railway in the UK covering some 25 miles (40 km) and taking 2¼ hours in duration. It travels from Caernarfon through impressive scenery before arriving at Porthmadog.
www.festrail.co.uk

PADARN LAKE RAILWAY

The 5 mile (8 km) return trip takes around an hour. *www.lake-railway.co.uk*

TALYLLYN RAILWAY

The Talyllyn journey starts at Tywyn wharf, the journey then continues to Abergynolwyn, the main inland station, before terminating at Nant Gwernol. *www.talyllyn.co.uk*

CORRIS RAILWAY

Situated between Dolgellau and Machynlleth in the Dulas Valley. Firmly established as one of the 'Great Little Trains of Wales'. *www.corris.co.uk*

Some slate mining and quarrying terminology

Adit: The entrance to a mine tunnel from the surface

Balanced incline: An incline with two railway tracks where the descent of the loaded wagons brought up the empty ones

Barracks: The accommodation area used by quarrymen usually through the week but occasionally all year

Black Powder: The original explosive used prior to dynamite

Block: A large piece of quarried slate

Blondin: A wire rope, supported by wooden towers, where a system of pulleys would raise, move and lower rock

Caban: A small shelter built from the waste rock by the miners normally used as a place of rest and at lunchtimes

Chain incline: A suspended incline using a wire rope instead of a railway line and inclined plane

Chamber: An underground working area that is up to 70 feet wide

Chwarel: The Welsh name for quarry

Cowjian: A plug chisel that is used for splitting blocks

Cup-boarding: This is the very dangerous practise of cutting into roofing pillars in order to get cheap or free slate

Cyllell: A long wide knife used to trim roofing slates to size

Drum: A horizontal drum around which the wire rope of a balanced incline was wound. Often made from wood

Fire-setting: A very old mining method used to weaken the slate by building a fire against a working face and then quenching with water. Going back almost 2,000 years it was described by Pliny the Elder in 77 AD

Floor: The working level of a quarry or mine and usually numbered

Ruined buildings at Rhosydd slate quarry near Blaenau ffestiniog

Jwmpah:	A long weighted rod weighted close to an end used for manually boring a holeLong weighted rod used to manually bore a hole. Used before the advent of compressed air drills
Launder:	A trough used for conveying water to a water wheel
Leat:	An artificial watercourse or aqueduct dug into the ground, especially one supplying water to a mill
Level:	Horizontal tunnel driven for access or drainage
Mill:	The building where slate is reduced by using machinery. At first water was used then latterly by electricity
Mine:	An underground excavation made to extract the slate. Quarry, pit and opencast are used for workings open to daylight
Pillar:	A column of slate left to support the roof above
Pillar robbing:	Same as cup-boarding
Plug and feathers:	A tool that consisted of two half round, tapered, short bars and a wedge. The two bars are inserted into a pre-drilled hole and then the wedge is hammered down between them, splitting the rock. Along with fire-setting, this was a common method of level driving before the introduction of gunpowder
Pric Mesur:	A serrated stick with nail in the end that was used to mark out roofing slate sizes
Quarry:	The distinction, in law, between a quarry and mine is somewhat unclear. The term quarry implies that the workings are open to the sky
Revetment:	A term used for a retaining wall
Rhys:	A large mallet used to break up large slate blocks
Rubbish:	The waste rock from the mining or quarrying process. It took around 10 tons of rock to produce 1 ton of usable slate
Shot hole:	The hole bored into the slate for the insertion of gunpowder
Strike:	A tunnel bored horizontally into the slate vein

Terrace:	A working level of an open quarry. These, like levels, were numbered
Un-topping:	The term used for removing the earth and rock from above the underground workings to remove pillars to gain cheap slate
Twll:	A surface pit working
Waliau:	Open fronted sheds where slate was hand trimmed and dressed
Water balance:	A type of incline where the weight of water was used to raise wagons.
Winding or Drum House:	This was built to support the winding mechanism at the head of an incline.

Drum house at the head of a Dinorwig incline

A selection of further reading

Exploring Snowdonia's Slate Heritage – 26 great walks by Des Marshall
ISBN 978-1-908748-52-2

Day Walks from the Slate Trail by Des Marshall
ISBN 978-1-84524-290-9

Snowdonia Slate Trail by Aled Owen
ISBN 978-1-898481-80-5

Gazetteer of Slate Quarrying in Wales by Alun John Richards
1SBN 1-84524-074-X

The Slate Railways of Wales by Alun John Richards
ISBN 0-86381-689-4

Welsh Slate Craft by Alun John Richards
ISBN 1-84527-029-0

Slate Quarrying in Corris by Alun John Richards
ISBN 1-84524-068-5

Slate Quarrying in Wales by Alun John Richards
1SBN 1-84527-026-6

Cwmorthin Slate Quarry by Graham Isherwood
ISBN 0-9522979-1-4

Rhiwbach Slate Quarry by Griff R Jones
ISBN 0-9533692-2-6

Welsh Slate by David Gwyn
ISBN 978 -1-871184-51-8

Dinorwic – The Llanberis Slate Quarry by Reg Chambers Jones
ISBN 978 – 1844940332

Slate from Abergynolwyn by Alan Holme, a member of the Talyllyn Preservation Society ISBN 978-0-9565652-4-2

Bryn Eglwys Slate Quarry by Alan Holmes and Sara Eade
ISBN 978-0-9565652-4-2

Rhosydd Quarry by M. J. T. Lewis
ISBN 078-1-9998134-2-0

Rhosydd – A personal view by Jean Napier
ISBN 0-86381-470-0

Within These Hills – A study of Corris Uchaf by Sara Eade
ISBN 978-0-9565652-1-1

The North Wales Quarrymen 1874–1922 by R. Merfyn Jones
ISBN 978-1-78316-175-1

A slate craftsman at the National Museum

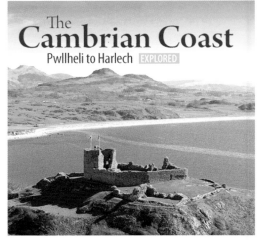

The Cambrian Coast
Pwllheli to Harlech EXPLORED

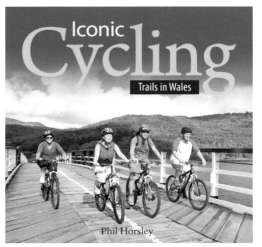

Iconic Cycling
Trails in Wales

Phil Horsley

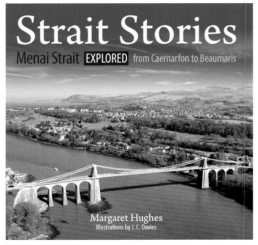

Strait Stories
Menai Strait EXPLORED from Caernarfon to Beaumaris

Margaret Hughes
Illustrations by J. C. Davies

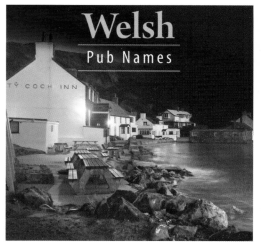

Welsh
Pub Names

TŶ COCH INN

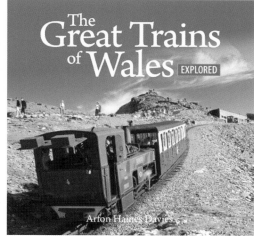

The
Great Trains
of Wales EXPLORED

Arfon Haines Davies

Snowdon
Villages and its
EXPLORED

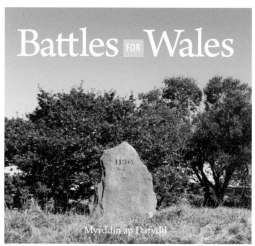

Battles FOR Wales

1136

Myrddin ap Dafydd

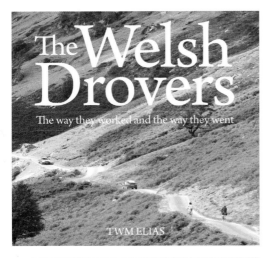

The Welsh Drovers

The way they worked and the way they went

TWM ELIAS

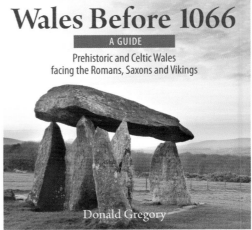

Wales Before 1066

A GUIDE

Prehistoric and Celtic Wales
facing the Romans, Saxons and Vikings

Donald Gregory

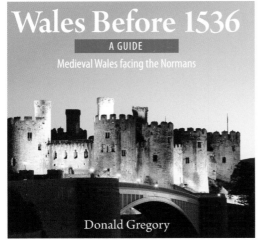

Wales Before 1536

A GUIDE

Medieval Wales facing the Normans

Donald Gregory

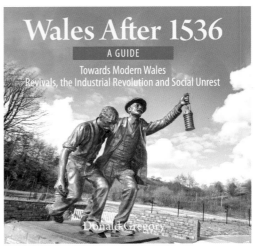

Wales After 1536

A GUIDE

Towards Modern Wales
Revivals, the Industrial Revolution and Social Unrest

Donald Gregory